Tweet poetry
#A poem A day

vol. #1

William Forchion

Dreamcatcher Entertainment, LLC
Brattleboro, VT 05301
www.dreamcatcherfilmworks.com

cover photo: Vincent Cotnoir © 2016
cover design: Dreamcatcher Entertainment,
LLC © 2018

        ISBN   978-0-9982978-1-1

For my mother
Eva Mitchell Forchion (1942 - 2018)

I am a flower of the garden of Eva,
as you see me blossom you share
the love the gardener poured into the
garden.

Introduction

During the month of April, national poetry month I began writing a poem a day, first thing in the morning, and posting them on twitter. Regularly I would share the day's poem with my mother during our morning phone call. I tasked myself to make it through the month. As the month concluded I decided to continue writing and tweeting. I did not give myself an end date, yet knew that I would take all poems I had written up to June 30th and publish them. On June 30th my mother died unexpectedly. In honor of my mother, who was my biggest fan and best friend, I publish this installment. Also in honor of my mother I will continue to write a poem a day until April 2019.

April 17

A mindless moment, neither now nor then, a projection of perfection, a shadow of an afterthought, a glimpse of the divine, time wraps around itself illuminating the soul.

#NPRpoetry #Billosophy #IAmEnough

April 18

Uncertainty remains constant, the unknown reveals itself as unknown, the answers lie within the answers, questions scrape the sky, fathoming the depths I weep, many many miles to go, unable to sleep.

#NPRpoetry #IAmEnough #Billosophy

The spectrum of grief spans from laugh to cry, offering no explanation for the emotional why, connection severed by non existing knife, is not the pain of death but the pain of life.

#NPRpoetry #IAmEnough #Billosophy

April 19

Instant everything, an all too brief eternity, an emotional spanicopita dripping with imagination, a never was and never again, this is now.

#NPRpoetry #IAmEnough #Billosophy

For generations my people's feet have not set in Africa, not even a toe, I'm not African- American I'm Black and I'm from Jersey, yo.

#NPRpoetry #aweebitsilly

April 20

Up pop the daffodils the tulips the
love, up pops the temperature as
the sun shines above, as life re-
emerges from the ground in the
spring, floral dreams come to col-
or and my soul needs to sing.

#NPRpoetry #IAmEnough #Billos-
ophy

April 21

Sunlight and shadow unconflicted
on the floor, springtime offering at
the altar just inside the garden
door.

#NPRpoetry #IAmEnough #Billos-
ophy

April 22

Strands of warmth permeate, kin-
dling - earth - heart - soul, sea-
sons change with life renewed,
the living cycle in divine control.

#NPRpoetry #IAmEnough #Billos-
ophy

In an ever changing world existence is transition, stasis feeds frustration anger jealousy, in acceptance of life's terminal condition, I love fully in order to celebrate me.

#NPRpoetry #IAmEnough #Billosophy

Anyone can critique, belittle, dis-
courage. It takes a soul connect-
ed to an unburdened heart that
knows freedom and is made of
pure love to inspire.

#IAmEnough #Billosophy
#livinginDreamtime #heart-
fulloflove

April 23

Sylvan silence, wrapped in bird-
song, shishle of leaves under foot
not mine, evidence of autumn
past, morning mindfulness, this is
now.

#NPRpoetry #IAmEnough #Billos-
ophy #livinginDreamtime

Step into the sunshine, let your flame burn setting the nearest star to blush, dance to the rhythm causing the gossiping to hush, sing the song only your heart knows, this is how you get paid what the universe owes.

#NPRpoetry #IAmEnough #Billosophy

April 24

Aroma fills the air of coffee
ground, brownies cupcakes cook-
ies scones, bodies in motion a city
of sound, a warm seat in the sun
to soothe my bones, with so many
choices an oatly chai restores my
health, ownership of moments like
this is how I measure wealth.

#NPRpoetry

April 25

Pitter pitter pat liquid life feeds
emerging flora, permeating
warmth awakens the solstice
sleepers, earth's aroma touches
multiple senses reminding the
heart to continue.

#NPRpoetry #NPRatc #IAmE-
nough #Billosophy

April 26

The leaf is me, alone on the tree,
awaiting my buds in spring.

#NPRpoetry #npratc #IAmEnough
#Billosophy

April 27

The divine enters, on rays of sunshine, in the song of birds, with
the breath of wind. With each cre-
ation the divine becomes again.

#NPRpoetry #IAmEnough #npratc
#Billosophy

Lost and confused a destination just off the map. Yet I know exactly where it is as I sit face in hands with elbows on my lap.

#NPRpoetry #IAmEnough #npratc #Billosophy

April 28

Broken walls are windows and doors, that's how the light flows. A caring soul unafraid to fail, that's how the love flows.

#NPRpoetry #IAmEnough #Billos-ophy #npratc

I was born without a dime.
Grandmama died owing more
than she ever made, what does it
cost to live? What does it cost to
love? Will there be an answer before I fade?

#NPRpoetry #blackpoet #IAmE-
nough

April 30

The space within is greater than
the thing itself, the unknowable far
exceeds the known, it is not hear-
ing or seeing that is accepting, it
is fully grasping the un-known

#NPRpoetry #iAmEnough #Billos-
ophy

With each blink the world outside
becomes new, everything has
shifted transforming all that is,
nothing remains constant except
the changes in me and you.

May 1

The entirety of life is transition,
just as bumps and bruises and
breaks will mend, the change is
constant in our place and posi-
tion, that which has begun will
eventually end.

#ApoemAday #IAmEnough

As the teacher, what I must do, is create an environment of learning that is physically and emotionally safe for you.

#ApoemAday #IAmEnough

May 2

With each new day dawns new
opportunities, new aromas to
smell new food to taste, fashioned
from our mind new worlds new
cities, bringing yesterday's sad-
ness and sorrow into this new
would be a waste.

#ApoemAday #IAmEnough

May 3

Embracing the divine is to know,
hope is not an action, being is as
powerful as doing, every law can
be broken or rewritten, miracles
occur regularly, Love never caus-
es hurt.

#ApoemAday #IAmEnough

May 4

Constant chatter as the mind
rambles on,
Fantasies and forgotten path float
in the same pool, amidst possible
solutions to impossibilities,
thoughts neither wild or control-
lable emerge.

#ApoemAday #IAmEnough

May 5

Time can be waisted, stretched, skipped, flown, compared and contrasted. There is one time like no other and that is time spent with friends.

May 6

Perspective shift, power trip,
imagination runs wild, technologi-
cal advances, cosmetic enhances,
political surprises, much the same
with age as when I was a child.

May 7

Life is somewhat precarious I may
only get one chance, there are
givens or guarantees for what I
am to do, when the spirit moves
me is when it's time to dance.

May 8

When the sunlight cradles the darkness and comforts it to sleep, the night dreams into life the day that is.

May 9

Wrestling thoughts similar to
pushing a rope, breathing and
thinking and doing day after day
after day, abandoning fear profit-
ing from hope, not the popular
path yet a purposeful way.

May 10

When the world becomes unbear-
able with frustration fear anger,
suit up in your garments of love
for they have no power in the
closet on the hanger.

#ApoemADay #IAmEnough #poet-
ry #VTpoet #unbottledgenie
#livingindreamtime

May 11

From head to toe with each heart
beat my soul vibrates like a bell
rings, from where I stand to the
limitless beyond my actions my
words my way is how the divine
sings.

#ApoemAday #IAmEnough #Bil-
losphy #poetry #VTpoet #livingin-
dreamtime #unbottledgenie

You are not an impostor you are
the true you as I am the one and
only me, don't let fear or ego or
the jealous ones tell you and me
otherwise, pour the love into you
to overflowing, now go on and be.

#IAmEnough #ApoemAday #poet-
ry #VTpoet #livingindreamtime
#unbottledgenie

May 12

Stand quietly, confident in stance,
think loudly, generating unique
opinion, drift effortlessly, pressing
persistently on the boundaries of
the possible.

Happy sad indifferent is a choice,
an opinion a mind crafted idea,
opinion and emotion become the
souls voice.

#weekendpoetry #VTpoet #poetry
#itaintallbeautiful

May 13

Planets in the galaxy like grasses
of the lawn, each a pixel in a photo universally vast.

#ApoemAday #IAmEnough #Bil-
losophy #poetry #VTpoet
#livingindreamtime #unbottledge-
nie

May 14

A million ideas a second popping
in and out of view, tell me what
your thinking, the space between
each thought considered, everything and nothing makes the answer true.

#ApoemAday #IAmEnough #poet-
ry #VTpoet #Billosophy #livingin-
dreamtime #unbottledgenie

May 15

The sun peeks over the horizon greeted by dawn sounds, the welcoming warmth of today gently caresses, a comforting quietness resonates from the treetops to the ground.

#ApoemAday #IAmEnough #Billosophy #poetry #VTpoet #livingindreamtime #unbottledgenie

Wipe my ego on the mat, remove the shoes, step inside, sunglasses off to receive the total brilliance of the soul, within is a universe that is home.

#poetry #IAmEnough #pocketpoems #Billosophy #unbottledgenie #livingindreamtime

May 16

In sylvan simplicity a moist blanket obscures the distance, encouraging my vision inward, the world races around time as it patiently waits, now is all there ever was.

May 17

Music helps me move, sitting
paused in meditation you may see
me at a glance, words flow in and
out and around me, they comfort
and soothe, the writing and the
poetry is the souls time to dance.

#ApoemAday #IAmEnough #poet-
ry #VTpoet #Billosophy #livingin-
dreamtime #amwriting

The words stumble out awkward-
ly, at best cumbersome beauty,
the prose disjointed stilted, best
guess this must be poetry.

#ApoemAday #IAmEnough
#amwriting #Billosophy #poetry
#livingindreamtime

May 18

We are not who we think we are,
we are capable of anything until
we constrict infinite possibility
with limited thought. Dream into
action.

#ApoemADay #IAmEnough
#amwriting #poetry #livingin-
dreamtime #VTpoet

Beautiful people and beautiful things are never in the way.

#IAmEnough #beautyeverywhere #FeelingFriday

May 19

In the moment we awake, the divine shall find rest, to constantly be alive within the dream is our only test.

#ApoemAday #IAmEnough #amwriting #Billosophy #livingindreamtime

May 20

Sunlight refracted through the prism of the soul, projects beautifully into the eyes of the viewer able to accept the divine.

#ApoemAday #IAmEnough #VT-poet #poetry #Billosophy #livingindreamtime #amwriting #SuperSoulSunday

When my soul was poured into this vessel I did not forget we were one, and will be again.

#SuperSoulSunday #IAmEnough #livingindreamtime #unbottledgenie #reikihealing #Billosophy #wrtingwithlight

May 21

In this moment all things hap-
pened, a universal ball of string
began then ended now, including
important and insignificant, this is
the only moment pertaining to
matter.

Remember when we were gorgeous and things were so good? In the future that will be today. Loving who I am and loving what is.

#billforchion.com #IAmEnough #livingrightnow #unbottledgenie

When I embrace loving me, I will know what it is to find my light.

#IAmEnough #Billosophy #billforchion.com

May 22

Sunlight yawns across the land-
scape, new life sings a waking
song, blossom scent the air, the
emerging day warmly kisses the
skin.

May 23

Life, birth to death, innocence to knowledge, hunger to nourishment, sleep to wake, a circle, we were young once and will be again.

The opposite of love is not hate, it is fear. Live into your loving lovable self.

#IAmEnough #Billosophy #truthwarrior #loveprophet #dreamtime #amwriting #inspirational #wokewednesday

May 24

One moment blurs into the next, I
breathe hope, I breathe love, in
and out, wake and sleep without
delineation, the magic is me, miracles abound.

It is easiest to put my faith in others when I first put my faith in me.

#IAmEnough #Billosophy #inspirational #motivation #trustme #faithful

May 25

I put on the day like a well worn
sock, familiar yet new, comforted
that the journey continues, excit-
ed and uncertain for what today
holds.

Violated victim, anger shame pain, me too is not my umbrella cause I'm a fella, baseless accusation accepted, bias on bias overlooking what was not, i accept no blame for what others did and I did not just because I'm a man.

We each have one story to tell, we tell that story in many parts, when the parts are all crafted and assembled there is the story of life.

#amwriting #IAmEnough #Billoso-phy #poetry #FeelGoodFriday

May 26

It is unreal what is real, what ap-
pears before me boggles the
mind, as what is in the mind mani-
fests itself outside, waking while
sleep then rising to live en-
wrapped in dream.

#ApoemAday #IAmEnough #poet-
ry #VTpoet

May 27

Little words, strung together, to
give meaning to enormous ideas,
vastness contained in a speck.

#ApoemAday #poetry

May 28

Atoms, aware of only the few
proximal neighbors, orbiting,
combining to create greatness, we
are.

#ApoemAday #IAmEnough #poet-
ry #Billosophy #VTpoet #Mindful-
Monday #divinity #amwriting #bill-
forchion.com

When I fill my heart with love
beauty surrounds me.

#IAmEnough #loving #Billosophy
#writeon

May 29

Softly floating between each step, enlivening the space between solids, daily we fly more than we fall, life is up and down and mostly in between.

May 30

Beyond man, beyond woman, un-filtered by shades, regardless of height and width and girth, we are human, we are one.

May 31

Words are only words until their
meaning transforms the reader.

June 1

Stand or sit, the power can not
hide, open, stay open, Love has
no need to hide.

#ApoemAday #IAmEnough #poet-
ry #amwriting #billforchion.com
#loveislove #livingindreamtime

June 2

Extend, the reach of my soul exceeds the length of my body, my
action becomes fantastic when I
accept the boundaries of the mind
are limitless.

#ApoemAday #IAmEnough #poet-
ry #amwriting #livingindreamtime
#inspirational #motivation #Billos-
ophy #writeon

June 3

Bent, shaped, distorted, repaired,
even our constants have variabili-
ty, allowing me to manage time.

June 4

Take each word, color it with love,
fill it with love, then release it to
the universe.

My uniqueness is a celebration for
all.

#IAmEnough #MotivationalMon-
day

June 5

What is seen, a reflection of what
is known, what is identified, on the
outside, is what has been cata-
logued, in the soul.

June 6

To dream is to kiss the divine.

#ApoemAday #IAmEnough #poetry #inspiration #Billosophy #wonderment #billforchion.com #amwriting

I remember you, in remembering you I remember me, yet I can not recall us, the divine lives in your smile, as I am reminded by my heart, as I breathe you in and out.

#poetry #writeon #IAmEnough #love #Billosophy #billforchion.-com #inspiration

There was a time I bathed in your light, we knew us, each a half of our whole, our oneness just right, together we were a song, that danced in our soul.

#poetry #latenitewriting #IAmEnough #ApoemAday #love #loving #divination #Billosophy #billforchion

June 7

Roots extend, attaching my soul
to the universe, pulse broadcast-
ing, morse code of existence, ra-
diating ripples, in the vast ocean
of the divine, finally awake, recog-
nizing home.

#ApoemAday #poetry #amwriting
#Billosophy #loving #love #inspi-
ration #billforchion.com #IAmE-
nough

One way to let go is to reach for something else.

June 8

Drinking in life, intoxicated to
staggering, needing more, knees
unstable, the option of return re-
moved, drink deeper, unlocking
the memory of this moment.

#ApoemAday #IAmEnough #poet-
ry #Billosophy #amwriting #divina-
tion #love

Miracles happen when inspiration exceeds limitations.

#IAmEnough #motivation #inspiration

June 9

Inhale, expiration, exhale, inspiration, the limitations of the possible, encapsulated in life's breath,
unburden potential, exceed expectation.

#ApoemAday #amwriting #poetry
#IAmEnough #Billosophy

I must first love myself before I can love another. I must first trust myself before I can trust another.

#IAmEnough #Billosophy #Motivation #inspiration #loving #trusting

June 10

Slowly purposefully I emerse myself, dipping below the waveless
surface, the last breath of this life
becomes the first breath of another, drinking in the divine.

#ApoemAday #poetry #IAmE-
nough

Proof of the divine surrounds me every moment.

#divineglory #IAmEnough #SuperSoulSunday #baskinginthespirit

June 11

An image refracted through a
crystal shard, light prismaticly re-
vealing its components, glimpses
of divinity.

June 12

My reflection, my projection, what
I think of me, neither true or false,
filtered fantasy of an active mind,
conjured illusion of pain desire
comfort pleasure.

Fear can be a masterful teacher when I am willing to learn.

#motivation #inspirational #wisdom #amwriting

June 13

Plummeting, into inky depths,
consumed by shadow I create, a
darkness in balance with my inner
light, falling becomes un-flight.

Light and Shadow, twin siblings,
of divine parentage.

Life is neither easy nor hard it just is. It seems to be what it isn't when we imagine it to be other than what it is. Removing expectation allows Life to be what it is.

#motivation #inspiration #IAmEnough #Igotthis #Billosophy

June 14

Two worlds, filled with love light
and the impossible, I fall into one,
I am pull back to the other, be-
longing in both and neither, each
day I purposefully enter awake
and asleep.

#ApoemAday #amwriting #IAmE-
nough #Billosophy #poetry

I must first dare to dream for that dream to ever become a reality.

#IAmEnough #motivation #inspiration #innerdrive #divinewisdom #wisdom #Billosophy

June 15

The day lay lifeless, I awoke and breathed life into it, magnificent colors filled in the shaded areas, it thanked me with beauty, it carried on as I drifted back to sleep.

#ApoemAday #IAmEnough #poetry #amwriting #Billosophy #sleep

June 16

Only I have the power to diminish
my light.

#shine #soulbright #IAmEnough

Neither good or bad, I stare into loving eyes, balance is black and white, and all the in between, this is who I am, the reflection and the me before the mirror.

June 17

You entered the world, and
changed me from man to father,
many diapers, many nights with
little sleep, first steps, first word,
many tears, pain and joy, father
became Dadda, Daddy and Dad.
Love

#ApoemAday #IAmEnough
#amwriting #poetry #Billosophy

June 18

Each day, an echo of the previous,
to be echoed in the next, subtle
nuanced additions, informing of
purpose, condensed vingnettes of
the entirety of a life.

#ApoemAday #poetry #IAmE-
nough #Billosophy

June 19

Surrounded, the joy and pain, that
is my world, directly connect, to
the contents of my soul, at times
discordantly, at times harmo-
niously.

#ApoemAday #poetry #Billosophy
#amwriting #writers #Thinkinga-
loud #IAmEnough

June 20

Safely curled into the folds of your
limbs, my soul nests in earshot of
your pulse, daily gathering and
hunting, I roam, returning to encapsulated security, smothered in
love, home.

June 21

Words milked slowly, from the
core, churned within the mind,
becoming butter, to be spread on
the page, then consumed by the
eyes, a poetic creamery.

June 22

When I open my mind and listen
with my heart and soul I am able
to hear nature.

#divinebeauty #Billosophy #IAm-
Enough #nature #amwriting #po-
etry #writeon #inspiration #weare-
one #love...

Words conveyed in deafening silence, meaning inferred in swirls and burls, strength signified with limbs outstretched, withstanding the tests of time, roots interconnected with all, arboreal presence.

#ApoemAday #amwriting #Billosophy #poetry #IAmEnough

June 23

Inhaling life, intoxicated on the essence of existence, exhaling, creating space within, consuming inspiration, preparation for the manifestation of miracles.

#ApoemAday #IAmEnough #Billosophy #writeon #amwriting #poetry #inspiration #miraclereadiness #indieauthor

June 24

Step out of the shadows, of fear and doubt, don the suit of trust, a suit of love, not armor, confidence stitched into each seam, soul suit, garment of the divine you.

#ApoemAday #IAmEnough #Billosophy #poetry #amwriting #indieauthors #writeon #SuperSoulSunday #inspirational

June 25

Radiance, experienced with gauzy
diffusion, highlighting spectral
anomalies, recognition of same-
ness, friend, family, synergy,
bound by the divine.

June 26

Standing on the the threshold, go-
ing back is not an option, yet
move I must, stepping into limitless possibilities, trusting, in self,
in the divine, miracles await, with
faith I go forth.

#ApoemAday #IAmEnough #Bil-
losophy #poetry #amwriting
#writeon #faith #inspirational

June 27

Silently scream into the darkness,
listening to a solo tear, gravitating
to the edge of the known face,
pleasure dozes peacefully, to
wake when enough is enough, as
the pendulum swings to extremes.

#ApoemAday #IAmEnough #poet-
ry #Billosophy #amwriting #writer-
slife #inspirational

June 28

Pouring forth from a sky bound
ocean, washing clean the unclean
in divine trust, none are immune
to the power, liquified heavenly
potion, drop by drop unto the un-
just and the just.

June 29

Proceed, respiration and circulation a constant, in motion, imagination un-impeded by fear, now is, future unknown, conjure miracles, embrace love, accept divinity, proceed.

#ApoemAday #IAmEnough #poetry #amwriting #Billosophy #divinity #inspirational

June 30

Individually we are candles burning bright, when we come together we combine our light, alone we light the face of, one boy, one girl, together we brighten the world.

#ApoemAday #IAmEnough #poetry #Billosophy #amwriting

July 1

Dear mom, long and Short has been you hair, through it all I knew you'd care, when I lost hope in a God above, it was through your loving I restored my love, you are no longer here my dear, yet I know you are everywhere.

#ApoemAday #lovingmom #IAm-Enough #Billosophy #greiving

About the author:

William Forchion brings his experience as a professional Clown, Acrobat, Stuntman and Voice performer to his thought provoking stream of consciousness writing. William can also be found traveling the world with his solo theater show "Billosophy: life ~ circus ~ death". His Billosophy podcast can be heard at www.theearspoon.com You can find out more about William at www.billforchion.com.

www.ingramcontent.com/pod-product-compliance
Lightning Source LLC
Chambersburg PA
CBHW061748020426
42331CB00006B/1397